I0158549

*between worlds*

# between worlds

POEMS

## Thomas Timmins

between worlds © 2021 Thomas Timmins
All rights reserved.

ISBN: 978-0-9975112-6-0

Published by Zoëtown® Media
Zoëtown is registered trademark of Zoëtown Media.
Greenfield, MA
www.thomastimmins.com

Cover art: Painting by Caraway Timmins

Book and cover design by Maureen Moore
Ginger Cat's Booksmyth Press
www.thebooksmythpress.com

*For Jasmin, Caraway, Joey, Danny*

# Contents

## Talking with ghosts

*Talking with ghosts*

## Flowers speak

I am the morning glory,
the sun's most perfect
mirror.

◆ ◆

I am the sunflower.
I bend my head
in honor,
father,
bowing to birds
that they may carry pieces of my soul
in their beaks and bellies
to all the hills and fields
exposed in the world.

◆ ◆

I am the magnolia.
My petals sail the wind's great river.
I am the soul's raft.
I carry the sins of the world
like babies on my silky skin.
I am the wild purple aster.
I stand up for trash dumped

on roadsides at night.
I adorn myself with dust spit by passing cars.
I praise chipmunk and mice hunters.
I offer my huge mauve heart
to fern shadows.

◆ ◆

I am the mushroom,
not plant, not animal.
I thank all green growing things
for their deaths.
I am the ghost of chlorophyll.
I am the resurrection of the felled pine.
I am the sweet bouquet of spring's
humiliation of winter,
the rank bouquet of autumn's
submission to the cold.

## Empty bird feeder

It's April and snowing.
We let the bird feeder hang empty
because we heard
there's a black bear awake,
prowling the neighborhood,
ravenous.

## Sound of a secret not yet shared

The shivering note
a bird's wings make
as it rises into the air.

## Stir crazy

April,
"the cruelest month,"
as cruel in 2020
as Eliot, the bank teller poet
imagined 100 years ago,
bitter cold and missing
the blesséd "shoures soote"
that Chaucer praised
700 years ago.

Today, far up in Maine,
just south of the borderline,
Yvette, worried,
said with a hopeful smile,
"Yeah, we're all
maskaholics nowadays.
Everybody's stir crazy
but see there?
A spattering of purple crocus
blooming in the snow."


*"shoures soote"* – Middle English for
"sweet showers" from Canterbury Tales

## Fairways in spring

The fairways in spring soak your feet.
Pinecones still on the branches refuse to fall.
The traffic on the highway stops, the sounds disappear.
My old mother, if she hadn't died, would celebrate
her birthday all day tomorrow.

Eight ladies and two men play-act
in improv class trying not to be dull
but it's cold in the house. They want to be close
to each other every Tuesday night.

Forget your desk, your laptop, your cells.
Recite new lines, dance and swing, dive off the pier
into black water. Onto the deck of the boat
the Captain hauls you in, hands you a towel.

You want to see your face
but all he has is a broken mirror.

## Hydrangea

A hydrangea bush blooming on the corner,
flooded with dowager pink blossoms,
tall as a cord of wood stacked high.

Another hydrangea flowing tree-like and
fountaining out.  Its flowers hang
like vigil candles surrounding
the empty grotto at its base.

Another hydrangea, flush and pink,
rising from the front yard like a cobra.

## May song

Shy trillium
bow their lustrous heads
on a rainy woodsy afternoon

offering walkers
who bend to peek
a sneak preview of earth's
blue eruptions

in violet petal

on indigo wing

in sapphire song.

## blue sky eye

sitting in my reading chair
not reading
staring southwest out the window
following the ancient practice

empty-headed
wondering about the salmon cloudhead
with the blue sky eye
planted square in the middle
of my window
ignoring the water streaks
through years of dust
smudging the storm window outside
ignoring the books and tablecloth
and candles and carnations and cards
propped across the tabletop
i forget what i was starting to think
oblivious to everything
except the blue sky eye
shining through my window
through my eyes
it feels peaceful
to ignore myself
and everything else
except the blue sky eye
beaming through the cloud

it's beginning to give me
a big slow joking wink
with its cumulus eye lids

and now it's gone

## The problem of life and death

is no problem.

Is a cycle.
a unicycle,
a bicycle,
a tri-quad-penta-multicycle,
then all of them at once until

when, all alone
we take the final spin
showing off a life of anti-grav
as it weaves and bobs
and bounces back and forth,
wheeling around the block
taking a last triumphant
hands-free, breeze-blasted ride

before we hop off and lie down
in the cool grass
to inhale the scent of wild
strawberries and fresh-mown hay
rising into the vault
of the cloud-strewn sky.

## Squirrels

The first,
smaller,
squirrel
scrambles up the sapling,
hops across the air
to the low branch,
stops,
wiggles its tail
waves it straight up
it undulates,
shimmies.

The second
squirrel
follows
up the sapling,
stops partway,
watches the first's
waggling tail
for a long few seconds,
then pivots
on its rear paws,
and skips
down to the earth.

The first squirrel
climbs quickly
to the other side
of the tree
where it sits,
alone,
scratching its ribs,
its tail drooped down,
still, soft,
rested  on a twig.

## Names of orchid children

| | |
|---|---|
| Why not | Dixie dust |
| Dark water | Victory |
| Oriental imp | Jewel box |
| Amazon trick | Le chit chat |
| Black stallion | Copper falls |
| Flower child | Long life |
| Charisma | Winter maiden |
| Golden everlasting | Starry eyes |
| Sweet memory | Red violet |
| Grand lady | Jungle cat |
| Babble | Beach Heaven |
| Lola | Black marble catnip |
| Golden eye | Golden daybreak |

Brother Supersonic

Desire at dawn

Doodle bug drag

Meeting house

Jerusalem jaunt

Tara town

Velvet caress

Teeth with antennae

Play all night

Love in the last pew

Come on over

Black hole

Amerigo frigate

Don't stop now

## Corn is the body of god

Corn is the body of god
whose ripeness and arid death
is our undisguised purpose

and pigs in their lolling
and meanness
are the body of god
whose spilled blood
causes our bellies to calm

and trees
whose gifts come seasonal
and year-round
are the body of god
whose life we expect
to last longer than ours.
But there are men
who in their old age
saw down trees,
tall, thick random trees,
and juicy shrubs,
just to cut them down.
For the men, outliving trees
is no small victory.

This god whose body
is corn and pigs and trees
alive in mud and sky,
dying to wind and steel
and time,
is also the body
of all mothers and fathers,

the Chlorophyll Mother
and Oxygen Mother
and Mother of Rock and Soil,
and the Snow Father
and Father of the Blade
whose children are
heat,
movement,
water,
from whom all children
of the first wandering cells
emerge,
to whom all children
dried to their final salts
dissolve.

## Western heat

I pedaled past the bison corral
in sweltering dusk.
One sign said "Bad Ground,"
the other "Danger Mad Buffalo."
I spotted him penned up
under the cottonwoods, pacing.

I'd be mad, too,
if they took my wives and calves
away and left me fenced in
with my sweat and shit
and wilting hay,
no roaming allowed my legs,
the trampled earth under my feet
grazed bare.

He seemed of normal bovine
intelligence, striding back and forth,
stirring up a cooling breeze
after the day of piercing sunlight
and  the 109 degree reading on the
"roller,"  the local cable TV's
 ceaseless weather report
rippling along the bottom
of the screen.

All normal weather here,
same as years past, the usual trial
for human and bison patience.

It's today's heat up in the bull's
homelands, somewhere near
the Black Hills where
the ranchers read 126
on thermometers,
but the good citizens in town
read 120, always underestimating
reality's grip in favor of
a balmy heaven.

The diligent ranchers
and these thick-necked bison
lie still for most of the day
into the evening now,
breathing slow.

## Fire walk


Last night,
    rain soaked,
        spun,
            tore,
                downed,
                    scarlet leaves.
                        all across town.


On this crisp sunny morning,
    I wish I were a crimson maple leaf
        twirling merrily
            between bough
            and ground.


That spinning leaf sensation,
    with nausea at first,
        bubbles fizzing in sinuses
        behind my eyes,
            a dizzy hint of exhilaration
            takes my breath.


My stomach twinges,
    my throat catches.

Then, suddenly, comes that
　　crystalline, silent
　　　　freedom of floating,
　　　　　　tacking crisp air
　　　　　　　　across a lazy, careless
　　　　　　　　　　yawn of sky.

Until, too soon,
　　I feel the bruising of leaf skin
　　　　slapped against stone on the ground.

Tiny slices by tough grass blades
　　rip reddening leaf flesh,
　　　　cutting soft tissue
　　　　　　where mighty chlorophyll drains.

In moments, the same drying
　　that wrinkles my forehead and face
　　　　begins to bake the fallen leaf.

The leaves still clinging to trees
　　glisten and glow,
　　　　pulsing yellow and orange embers
　　　　　about to engulf whole trees
　　　　　　　from their branches down.

I see now
　　how anyone can walk on fire:

Shuffle across the lawn
    at noon
        under scarlet Norway maples
           on a sunny late-October day
           scuffing through leaves.

Your feet crackle
and singe,
      kindled
          by sizzling earth.

## Coyote

Just as I looked up from the deck,
a flock of shiny juncos flew off.
Then the black squirrel
nuzzling for seeds in the yard
shot away, leaping across a fallen tree
and up into the branches of a hemlock.

A coyote appeared, solo, muscled,
wearing buff, red, brown, black and white fur,
stopped for a few seconds,
ears cocked, nose up,
then dashed off into the trees down the hill.

Soon, it was sunset.
Then, night, that dangerous time,
dropped into the woods, wearing silence.

## Mask

*for Caraway*

I poured my whole self
into making the mask.

I dug the clay
from a shady hillside spot
near Black's pond on dad's farm.

The flames for his hair
I found in my sister's old drawings.

I sharpened his teeth to match
the fire blazing off his skull.

I tried to make him fierce,
terrible, but he kept smiling.

So I squeezed his mouth
and pulled his lips back.
I narrowed his eyes
and pointed his nose down.

I used a terra cotta glaze
but the kiln held him longer
and hotter than I wanted.
He's deep red,
the red at the heart of slow burning oak.

When I heard my friend say,
"That really looks evil,"
I knew I had him.

## October trees know sadness

Maples weep untold anger.

Oaks cry hidden bruises.

Hickory peel away grief.

Birch wail untold dreams.

Beech reveal clinging fears.

The whole forest pours down endless mourning.

All the leaves pool in the wetness of sorrow.

## Lightning bolts

Hot sheet
      Lemon splash
           Sky render
                Sky writer
           Sky rider
      Dazzling thorn
Sky flame
      Whip of fire
           Deadly bush
                Night's master
                    Day's tease
                Silver amulet
           Wrath of god
      Fury's dagger
Sky slit
      Bloody eye
           Burning roots
      Blazing tree
Night's fangs
      Slashing tree

## Ardor

In the mountains last night,
far across the land we call our country,
first frost settled on the parsley,
ice-burning the tender plants in Janina's garden.

Alert, expectant, we await the snow while today
the neighbor's chimney exhales the odor
of newspaper ash and scorched green wood sap.
When the true cold comes, he'll burn
dry fragrant logs his wife sawed and,

panting and huffing,
heaved and stacked before she left town
hoping her woodpile ardor
will keep him warm through the winter.
All of our heat depends on the air we breathe.

## Last to first frost

leaping from the grass,
    frost bites my ankles —
        barefoot stroll in April dawn

shaking the petals
    like a dog's jaws ripping meat,
        the butterfly feeds

the rainiest June —
    ducks swim blue water
        among green corn shoots

hiking a steamy hill
    swimming through July —
        a two-legged bass

rustling a pale herd
    of cottonwood leaves,
        outlaw autumn gallops in

chilling in September sun,
    I lie down on moss —
        wind soughs, crickets throb

roadside painter says
        "Work from dark to light. How else find
           all the values of things?"

on the woods road,
        swollen worms, sluggish newts —
           autumn rain showers

shirtless, wearing shorts, sandals.
        shivering, I take out the trash —
           last night of summer

kneeling in the road, she reaches,
        fingers gently snatch —
           toad  safety patrol

walking fast, talking,
        she lifts up her shirt for breeze —
           her round brown belly glows

first we spent too much,
        then we gave too little —
           money comes, love goes

her warm breast crushed
        against the back of my thigh —
           massage therapy

first date, she's late —
       clouds spill east, porch swing rattles —
           o well ...  good book tonight

shaggy hundred-year maple
       wears headstones like ears —
           backwoods cemetery

kitchen boss's eyes flashing,
       hands soaking, she laughs —
           dancing with dishes

orange lights flash in sunshine
       sinking into brown dirt —
           ploughed-in pumpkins

golden leaves skirl past
       my dusty window —
           uh oh, the pane's cracked

bare trees, crickets sing,
       shirt off, I lounge on the beach —
           October heat wave

first frost's vapors
       skimmed light pouring over the valley —
           November morning

## Northern luxury

A bed
warm enough
in winter

to sleep in
with my clothes
off.

## Bonfire

*for Danny*

Again it's come time
to celebrate the end
of the darkening days
of the calendar
while letting pass by
the dark days of humans,
those who ignore the seasons
because time means nothing
to them whose hearts
dredge the dark.

Among us, we
who are stained
by our own losses
and ignorance
and even hate for those
we deem weaker,
we who've missed
offering simple kindness
to a child or person in pain,
who've missed
receiving
simple kindness
again and again,
so we feel weak
and forgotten.

Then maybe someday,
maybe now in summer,
just past dawn,
then in tree-dappled noon,
then at the sighing edge
of twilight,
we find ourselves outside
beside a bonfire,
warming ourselves
in the gift of flicking light,
staring again and again
into the wavering flames,
inhaling fragrant smoke
that rises half shadow,
half dusky sky,

until later,
when we close our eyes
against the winking embers
and raise ourselves
and murmur good-bye
or good night
and go.

## The good luck

Home after midnight I was not
out catting around
anymore than I was boozing
or gambling,
tho I had a Kingfisher beer
with my mixed Tandoori grill
while talking business with Laxman
the chef and owner
agreeing that sometimes
you have to roll the dice.

I resisted telling him I knew a god
who gallivants across the earth
in one hand a pair of dice
in the other red silk lingerie,
his or his lover's?
that's the mystery to ponder,
the dice we recognize
from children's board games
and fluffy rear view mirror mobiles
to institutionalized losing
on somebody else's turf and terms.

The odds always favor house
in the long run I said

Then the gambler who wants to win Laxman
said gets inside the house, better yet he owns it
and rolls the dice across his own tables

Don't forget luck, I reminded him
Luck has more power than any house

You mean the good luck he said

Yeah the good luck

the good American luck that won the ranch
that built the herds
that sent the son to school in the east  and
down to Congress
to win the land and water rights for the ranch
that covered half the state

That's the kind of luck I always have he said
only in my way
When I lost my first restaurant
that was good luck
because here I am now,
making money every day

Maybe lucky gamblers change history I said
but what if you'd lost
your next restaurant?

I didn't he said

What about the future?

I won't he said ordering another beer
for himself

There's no such thing anyway, I said,
as the future.

No, he agreed, we say
take care of the grass
in your field today, don't worry
about the milk in your cup tomorrow

In that case, my friend, I said,
pulling out my deck
of worn blue Bicycle cards,
let's draw

OK, he said if we use these too, he smiled,
extracting from his pocket
a pair of weathered yellow dice
whose eyes had worn to amber
in their sockets  Let's see
who lady luck loves tonight he said

What's the bet? I said

Pick a card I said

Roll them bones he said

## Talking with ghosts

running up the hill
for pleasure — the pain,
old man's bane, athlete's disdain

all of us end up
at the station where all
trains come in — when do they depart?

leaving commune house,
dropping out of group,
my job — find stones lit inside

can't breathe in white car,
windows won't roll down — can't do it alone

who is this i
going solo now?
dark buildings glow in my hands

smoking cigarette
telling my chef friend,
can't stick around here — go, he says

little actress down the street
turns hummer-size wagon
under trees, circles the house

i drive old home streets, alone,
until three spirits jump in  —
where to, boys?

they don't speak, they don't
turn to look at me,
gray, fuzzed  — no scent

you guys want to talk
or you just gonna
sit there, spooking me out? speak

we're your pals, your
deepest wishes, genies
in the dreamworld, you see that

don't bullshit me with
genie-wish-come-true
garbage, it's too tempting

try us, we're the ones,
cosmic helpers, we've
watched you years, now you see us

tell me this: how fast
will my dreams come true?
depends on the dream, my friend

did my friend send you
or did my hunger
for love incant? and why three?

triumvirates last,
with you we're a solid four —
watch out, your headlights barely shine

we're watching your back
we're singing your song,
hotshot grace, riding along

three cloudy bodies
riding in my car
no voice, no names  —  good or bad?

## America, a resurrection song

America, America, America,
you used to be somebody.

People talked to you
when they needed help.
Singers sang about you
and your irresistible beauties.
Choruses of longing rose from the hearts
of your beloved crowds.
Famous poets believed you
worthy of poetry.
They promised they would
touch you in the heart
with their praise and hope.

They couldn't say that nowadays
because you've lost your heart.
In fact, you have no body.
Even if I were speaking to you right now,
how could you hear me
without ears?

I'm not speaking to you, America.

If I were, and if somebody
overheard me, they'd wonder
if that man had mental problems.

I may be mad,
who isn't these days?
Just look at who believes in America,
the Santa Claus
of the Globalcorp
sailing through the sooty clouds.

There is a body here –
it's billions of humans
and their animals and plants
and the wilds –
but America, you are a giant
without a body.
You're still an idea,
a spiritual being,
a ghost of dreams past and future,
a spirit set free to inflame
the human heart.

I am Thomas, the doubter.
I try to feel you still here,
but you have no flesh.

You can't feel the wind or the rain.
You don't eat. You don't shit.
When I listen deeply,
I hear scraping and groaning.

A fetid smell rises from rain-bowed slicks
on the edge of roads.
Something's skunking up

the Atlantic shores.
Where's your deodorant
of fresh air, America?

America, you are the name,
the pledge of democracy.
You are the name
for a place of opportunity,
but you lost your reputation
in a casino where
our needy elders pull and pull
and lose and lose
until they feel the barren spurt of
ka-ching, ka-ching, ka-ching.

Your name once had synonyms
that wore their capital letters
like prayer flags.
Synonyms like 'Freedom,' 'Justice,'
'Dreams Come True.'

Now your synonyms are
brand names that don't need
a little poem to join their
self-promoting cavalcade
of advertisements and disinformations.

But O, those images of
ineffable beauty,
fast moving metallic potency,
the softest of nights

where peace and silence
offer dreamless sleep in
the afterlife of TV's
soapy glories and fears,
who can resist those?

America, are you now really
just a name
afloat in the past,
a name that once mantled us
like wings of light?

Now your mantle hangs
off your shoulders
like a shroud,
the violent cape of Captain Grief.
Do you love your cape
because it casts a shadow
all around you, a moat
you can wear around
your crumbled castle
like a necklace of crocodiles
and whips and nooses
and missiles and human skulls,
a devotee of the goddess Kali,
the mother of radiation, mutation, incineration?

Our role now?
Stay out of your way,
escape your shadow,
and let you fall down into

the rock bottom rust and ash
when maybe then you can decide
not to give up and arise because
so many gave up on you
and you, like us,
dream freedom and presence.

You used to be a family
where we cared for each other
just because we were
brothers, sisters, cousins,
even grouchy neighbors
we didn't want to
but we did help.

You were a refuge
for the lost and lonely.

Now we're refugees
locked inside the crowded camp
of your borders.

What can we do?
Can we raise up a wind of laughing
and shouting to blow away that shroud?

If the shroud's too heavy
for our breath to lift,
we can light a million candles
and burn it
to free you from the weight.

Then we'll run
from the flaming shreds
and embers raining down
on a land with no name.

America, I know your old name
lives on in the ground
within this world
where real people surf past it
like a movie made for TV.
The trailers promised
an explosion at the end
of a hair-raising chase
while the sponsors insisted
on happy endings,
no matter what.

America,
you used to be somebody,
and if I don't want you
to disappear into
the empty synapses of history,
I'll have to practice
the mourning rituals,
wail for seven days and nights
then turn around
and around
and around again
until I'm dizzy and high
and even then you
might be gone.

Ah, the shame of it.
The pity of it.

But who needs a name
if you stay unborn?

For so long now,
I've watched you
reach into your top hat,
swish your fingers around
and pull out a rabbit stuffed
with possibility for the kids,
or a winning Super Lotto ticket
for the desperate,
or a gift card that says
with a big grin,
"Bearer Entitled to Share
in the Common Green."

You must earn your name now.
All the tears
flowing down your hollow cheeks
into your sagging mouth
mumbling self-talk like 'war is good
and we're the winners',
'rich is what we are,'
'jail is for you, not for me.'

O, America, in your suffering
you're drenched in cruel beauty
and still you call me to love you.

In my canine despair
I hear the call
and call back to you.

Please listen to this sad little
resurrection song.
I raise it above the crash
of endless traffic on the coasts where, deny-
ing jellyfish blooms
and the rank scents
seeping from the shores,

all the people in their driver's seats
aim straight ahead,
going somewhere,
not seeing past their blind spots
the slow rising of the tides.

America, I'm always trying
to clear the air between us.
I'll shout, sing, nudge you
like a brother who knows
you can do it.

So let the tides swell, the smoke rise,
our people stop
and lay down confused.

I and I and all of us wait,
not in our dreams or hopes,
but in our bodies

washed in the blood
and baptized in the miracles
of our children's children's children.

It's not too late for us
to feel joy and even euphoria
as our due,
now and always,

as we wait for you to emerge
into the flesh,
your pride shining from
limpid, caring eyes,
with your heart aching
from missing us
and returning to our
open arms.

## Hullaballoo
*for Joey*

A hullabaloo
wants to erupt from these words.
At first, it only leaks a warning:
look here.
Then, it shouts:
Stand back,
stand back.
Pop up your umbrella.
Now,
you courageous and careless –
you know who you are –
say the word
"hullaballoo" aloud.
Now.
Say it slow.
Hulla
balloo.
Draw out the syllables.
Call them forth into
the peal of the world.
Hear them somersault
and roll
and pirouette
on round-toed shoes.
Hulla
balloo.
Hullaballoo. Hullaballoo.

*Louis Armstrong*

## Ontario clouds

Ozonated days linger halfway to the top of Ontario where the sky ripples with clouds reflecting clouds from the lakes below where they began as waves licking at a breezy day, like the day we creased the map at the line demarcating the Arctic watershed and crossed over on the family adventure into a story wilder than a story about the gold miner cousins.

As usual, the older kids left at dawn to chase rainbows while the younger stayed home, quilting clouds, barns, bears, and lakes. Walter, the youngest at thirteen, managed to crochet a California Golden Eagle, using purple and red thread.

Its dramatic hues appealed to Ronni, the head rainbow hunter who was color blind but she identified that unmistakable Golden Eagle beak.

"Nice," Ronni said, fondling the raptor's fabric silhouette laid across her knee. "Why don't you knit us a flock of them Eagles so we can sneak up on the rainbows from above."

Ronni sat down while Walt set to work and the vast herd of albino cumulus collapsed into the lakes where they spend the night as insomniac white caps.

A north country rumor has it that its clouds dream in the lake beds until dawn all the plots and slippery characters they'll perform when they rise for tomorrow's spectacle racing scene by breathless scene above Ontario's north-flowing waters.

The best seats in the house, the canoes and rafts, are never sold out.

**Pacific coastal winds**

1.

Waves mediate between wind and currents. Wind makes waves and waves affect currents, intermixing and changing with undersea life patterns.

Wind and waves interact to complete a cycle: currents affect the air temperature which causes winds which pushes and pulls rains and sends the water back to the seas that wait, receiving water, wind, heat, material in the air and in the water, in service of the planet as a kind of digestion.

Some materials immediately nourish fish and vegetable and some return to the air, bolstering new weather. The sea excretes most spent life forms to the sea bottom where they can cure, compost, metastasize, transform, or disappear under the alchemical weight of the ocean.

## 2.

Nervous as flutters of emotion across dreaming psyches, fitful winds rise just before sunrise out of pools of shadows and mist sunk into hollows, dampening the necks and wings of little birds sleeping in the bushes.

Cool uncertain soughs circulate through the shady morning canyons before the heat of day draws them up and away from their lollygagging among low branches, flattening and spreading them across the mountainside where some drift off, diminishing into warm puffs and gentle gusts hummingbirds batter with their drumming wings.

Some of the tentative zephyrs huddle together, riding larger breezes as they swirl, radiating nebulous lassoes of pressure like arms gathering wafts into sizable drafts, searching for stability within the dissolving waves of heat and fine steam released by plants into magnetic blue morning sunlight.

The breezes coalesce into massive updrafts turkey vultures sail on with their gnarled red wattles crimped under necks bent down, their eyes scavenging for fresh scraps putrefying in sun or shade after night's skirmishes in the brush on the tops of the dunes.

## A small beach cave

I'm hiding from the mid-day sun in a cave in a bluff a few yards from the Pacific.

The size of a small bedroom, the cave faces south into a rising blue tide and a harsh yellow sky. Every gull I've watched fly by has flown south, into the light wind. One rebel cormorant arrowed swiftly downwind, its ebony wingtips nearly brushing the foam. A few sailboats tilt across the water beyond the floating brown kelp gardens.

At the cave's back, where the walls funnel down to the sand floor, a section of wall seeps under a blanket of chartreuse and russet and mustard mosses. I suppose it's the source of the cave, the leakage having weakened part of the bluff to the tide's ruthless coring. A faint but persistent odor of sulfur drifts toward the cave mouth.

Wide striations of gray clay compressed into roughly square blocks that fit together like badly laid tiles form the walls of the cave. I'm surprised that not even a smudge of the oil that bubbles out of the ocean floor here grafittis the walls with its Paleozoic shadow.

Dozens of sharp chunks of cave wall and ceiling lay half-buried in the sand shelf I sit on. They litter the floor like New England rocks abrupted into abandoned fields, useless for building stone walls or fireplaces. As the bluff crumbles into beach, a beebee of the ceiling falls onto my bare knee, a splash of fine gray silica. I tip my cap down over my eyes, lean back, and nap.

## Lupine

On late March afternoons, swarms of purple lupine lounge on the grasses like seraglios picnicking.

All over these wanton hillsides, the modest cattle, preferring to ruminate undistracted by beauty, avoid the tiny forests of flowers, while the lecherous sunlight stumbles headlong through oak shadows, angling for the perfect sensual slant to sprawl across sapphire blossoms whose vulval petals drive the sky itself crazy with desire.

## Louis Armstrong

A four-foot tall watercolor painting
framed in glass in a thin wood
frame painted black and
tarnished gold.  Louis Armstrong,
large, proud, brown,
dressed in black tie and tails,
arms thrown wide open
to a scarlet sky
or red velvet stage drape.

In one hand, a proper
derby hat floats, in the other,
shaped like the club in a deck of
cards, with a handle like a ping
pong paddle, a yellow flower fan,
fluffy as a hydrangea blossom. He
wears a red and yellow banner
draped from left shoulder across
his heart down to right hip. A
globe of yellow flower,
the same as the fan, blooming as
large as his head perches on his
shoulder, like a dangling giant
carnation earring.

He raises his chin, turns his lips down and solemn. He closes his eyes and opens his whole body – feet splayed, big strong belly rumpling his white shirt – and holds it still, invoking into the silence the ancient spirits of music, dance, freedom.

Over his head, the golden words "New Orleans" gleam. The "O" hangs from the point of the "N" like a horseshoe on a barn nail, a bubble of light anchored to the "N" that would drift off if the "N" hadn't hooked it like a lucky angler.

In the seams between the frame and glass, circling the man in an old moon crescent on three sides, leaving the top open to the sky, I stuffed photos of my children from their childhoods to their young adulthoods. Outdoor shots of camping in mountain wilderness, shots of lounging on chairs indoors, reading, sleeping.

Obscuring the parade
master's knees and words that
say "Heritage and Jazz Festival"
but revealing the letter "J,"
curlicued and doubled into a
treble clef sign, I taped on the
glass two notes to myself — one
about how to start a novel and to
tell a great story, clues from the
teachers like "Start as close to the
end as possible" and the other, a
reminder to work every day.

I switch the photos around
depending on how I feel any day
and which kids are doing what,
who wants to play frisbee or sit
reading or stir the lake water or
grin from behind sunglasses or
make a sandwich on the picnic
table. If I listen closely, I hear
horns and drums and waterfalls. I
watch the poster and my feet start
tapping. Before I know it, I'm
standing up, swinging around the
room, snapping my fingers,
dancing with my chair,
the beloveds of all my life
dancing with me
in the air.

*between worlds*

## Liminal

During the longest period of our awareness, we're between the unknowns before birth and after death.

During our shortest intervals, every instant happens between the past and the future.

The word for this in-betweenness where we live is *liminal,* at the threshold. It's both a time and a place – a time before we act anew, a mental place where uncertainty rules.

The liminal can feel dangerous because we can't go back in space or time and whatever we do or don't do, we find ourselves in the unknown.

Or, the liminal can feel comfortable once we accept the unknown as the way it is.

## Luck

Luck,
and other events of the microcosm
like desire,
like death,
resists human control,
tho, lord knows,
we try.

## Work

When I work,
I profess my faith
in the power of longing
to prevent myself
from succumbing
to what is.

## Lost in the brain

*for my bro Joe*

Out here in the part of the brain
where dreams flow against the grain,
where thoughts and feelings first entrain,
an incandescent flame blows the main.

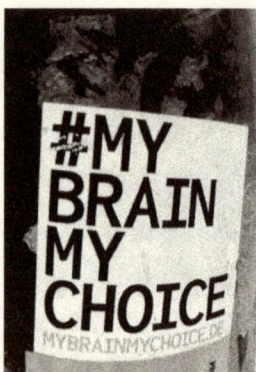

## Sue Mac and Willow
*for Jasmin*

Sue Mac met Willow
along the riverbank.

Hooting,
thudding down the rails,
the Montreal Express sang their ode:

Twoooo hearts
Twoooo hearts
Freeeee hearts

Willow's lean tall frame
bent around Sue.
She pinked.
She rose in his arms,
a cluster of wings.

Sue reddened.
Willow swayed.

The train's fadaway howl
whispered around them,
an afternoon sigh.

## Bliss

*for Amy*

Late afternoon light
danced on turquoise water
as we floated
on mother of pearl air.

The forest burned plum.

Green shadows
soothed our jaws,
tender from so much talking
and kissing.

## Her new series

This is so good, she says
of her new series,
I can't stop watching.
If your light is still on
when the show's over,
I'll come in to say good night.
He smiles and yawns.

## Dessert

You say
you don't like
my poems

but I love
your pecan pie.

## Good thing, bad thing

It's good to know
the way to your house.

The bad thing is
not to know
when to go home.

## Why worry about the slippery streets

Why do we care
about ice on the roads
and sidewalks
when in this town
with so many churches,
and with living saints
next door
and all across town
who get down on their knees
for us
every day?

## Patience

Wind creeps and sighs,
urging old sandbars
that refuse to budge,
even as the tides flow.

Wind sends its rakes
slashing across boulders,
cultivating granite fields
with sandy tines.

This goes on for years, eons.

Imagine
the utter freedom
from time
the wind bears
in its constant, patient arms.

### "Livin the dream"

Summer evening.
His fishing lines
adrift in the slow river.
His barelegged girlfriend
sets a bonfire on the sand.

As I pass by on the road,
I call, "How ya doin?"

"Livin the dream," he says.
"Livin the dream."

## Illusion

The illusion
that the fallen leaf
is separate
from the ripe flesh
of the plum
or the pit,
the single-minded missionary
of the root.

## Homecoming

After the movies,
after the game,
after the party,

home invites us
like the fragrance
of a night-blooming jasmine

when in February
we stepped off the plane
from Boston to San Juan.

## Down in the cellar

The channel running
under our old house
flows through granite stone,
a smooth lightless stream.

Down in the cellar
we open a door,
a door in the floor.

We lower our pails,
and raise them up slow.
The water tastes sweet
and rich, like chilled cream.

## The sink is crying

The sink is crying
and the soap doesn't care.

The soap has one desire:
to be touched, picked up, fondled, used,
worn away in love with skin.
Since soap can never be skin,
it always feels a little sad.

The sink is crying
because the soap is dripping
in its ecstatic going,
and the sink is afraid
it will dry up
under the mirror's cool light
and never again attract fingers and palms,
even to rinse away smudges,
even to fill an empty cup,
even to wet thirsty lips.

## Along all the rivers

A wind blew all night
along all the rivers and streams
of the world
raising mist into the sky
and floating my dreams
through thick fog
that dimmed the stars
from my memory.

## Black and white

There on the wall,
deep in shadow,
black and white,
not much gray.

You said, is that
a painting? A photo?

We stared from the bed.
The house was quiet.
It was nearly dusk.

It's lovely, you said.

Yes, I said,
beautiful.
You see snow
weighing down hemlock boughs.
You're looking through the window.

## Success

I never learned
to play chess
or build complex
Lego creatures.

Because of that
& some other reasons,
I'm still working
on being ... what's it called?
A success.

Lately, love
exalts my days & nights.

No working needed.
Lucky me.

## Choice in the canyon

down in the canyons
under smooth cliff walls
my world shrinks
to a stream rushing

between the temptation
to find a ledge
by the water
to stretch out and doze
in the shade

or take the lure
of the chancey climb
up dark seams
to the sun
at the top?

## Retirement plan

Love with all the madness I can
Make and keep deep friends
Meander in beautiful places
Enjoy all the verve earth offers

Write and learn
and read and dream
and walk and talk and play

until the last wave of daylight
finally breaks over my head
& I succumb to nature's need
to have my atoms back

## Languages of winter

Look up into the trees
where the naked branches
write all across the sky
the word "light"
in a million languages
every one of which
we speak
in our mother tongue.

## Hawk

When a hawk flies low and close
across the December sky in front of me,
I'm tempted to and do believe I receive a message.

The essence of the message is the sudden presence
of a wild silence in flight. It's like, and maybe it is,
a visitation from an angel.

Of course, a real angel visited the Virgin
after forming its soul into a physical being
with a voice, a winged creature in the flesh
she could see and hear and believe.

And aren't we such beings with souls
who sometimes attract spirits who speak to us,
inviting us to bear our tender gods
into this world of dreams and flight?

# The longings of ice

Old wife
of the hoary logger,

pregnant
again
by his faithful seed
since summer's end,

the February river
lies swollen
and still

dreaming
of sailing
winged mangoes
through the sultry nimbus
of the moon.

## between worlds

I slept deeply, on and on,
finally waking
in a lightless place

where travelers stayed still
while new people and lands
came to meet them

before passing on
without leaving
even a trace of shadow.

Caisleáin Dhun Guaire  County Galway, Ireland.
Dunguaire Castle.

*Dhun* is a fort.  *Guaraire* is the name of a king from the 7th century.  Family lore says the Timmins ancestors helped build this castle

www.ingramcontent.com/pod-product-compliance
Lightning Source LLC
Chambersburg PA
CBHW021934040426
42448CB00008B/1063